Encyclopedia of Peg Saints

By Maggie & Michael Jetty

Agnes ~ Page 2
Thomas Aquinas ~ Page 3
John Bosco ~ Page 4
Blaise ~ Page 5
Katherine Drexel ~ Page 6
Dominic Savio ~ Page 7
Patrick ~ Page 8
Francis Paola ~ Page 9
Gemma Galgani ~ Page 10
Mark ~ Page 11
Our Lady of Fatima ~ Page 12
Dymphna ~ 13

Joan of Arc ~ Page 14
Anthony ~ Page 15
Maria Goretti ~ Page 16
Benedict ~ Page 17
Veronica ~ Page 18
Kateri ~ Page 19
Mary Magdalene ~ Page 20
James ~ Page 21

Christopher ~ Page 22
Ignatius ~ Page 23
John Vianney ~ Page 24
Monica ~ Page 25
Mother Teresa ~ Page 26
Padre Pio ~ Page 27
Gabriel ~ Page 28
Michael ~ Page 29
Therese of Lisieux ~ Page 30
Francis of Assisi ~ Page 31
Teresa of Avila ~ Page 32
John Paul II ~ Page 33
Juan Diego ~ Page 34
Our Lady of Guadalupe ~ Page 35
Lucy ~ Page 36
John the Evangelist ~ Page 37

CARITAS PRESS

ST. AGNES OF ROME
Feast Day January 21

St. Agnes
Birth: January 28, 292 in Rome, Italy
Death: 304 in Rome, Italy

Agnes lived in Rome during the time of pagan leaders. The son of a pagan governor was upset when Agnes refused to marry him. She desired to live a life of purity and chastity for Christ. The governor ordered her to abandon her faith and marry his son. Even though he threatened her with death, Agnes refused. She died a Christian martyr.

Patron saint of of girls, gardeners, chastity, engaged couples, and Children of Mary.

She was seen smiling joyfully even when people were mean to her. She did not fear death because she knew that if she died for Jesus, she would be united with Him in heaven. She was excited to go to heaven.

"Christ made my soul beautiful with the jewels of grace and virtue. I belong to Him whom the angels serve."
-St. Agnes

Crown of flowers, a symbol of purity

Her name in Spanish is "Ines"

A lamb is a symbol of Christ. Every year on Agnes' feast day, the pope blesses a pair of lambs whose wool is used for the palliums, the stoles worn by Archbishops over their chasibles in the shape of the letter "Y."

In Greek, her name means "pure". In Latin, it means "lamb."

Palm branches are a symbol of martyrdom.

Agnes was watched over by her angel. When the governor sent Agnes to an unsafe place, she was protected from all dangers. On another occasion she walked away unharmed after the governor had her thrown in a fire!

In Rome, a church is named in her honor and a relic of her skull is preserved in a special chapel within the church.

2

St. Thomas Aquinas

Birth: January 28, 1225, Roccasecca, Italy
Death: March 7, 1274, Fossanova, Italy
Canonized: 1323 by Pope Pius V

Thomas was a gifted student from a very young age. He excelled in school and in practicing virtues. He desired to be a priest from the order of St. Dominic. His noble family wanted him to marry instead of becoming a Dominican Friar and tempted him by introducing him to beautiful women, but God blessed him with the gift of perfect chastity and he was able to focus on dedicating his life to Christ as a priest.

ST. THOMAS AQUINAS
Feast Day January 28

- Patron saint of education, universities, students, publishers, & theologians
- Nickname: "Angelic Doctor" or "Angelic Thomas" because of his great purity and his expertise in his writings on the angels.
- He studied at universities in Cologne, Germany, and Paris, France.
- He is a Doctor of the Church because of his influential writings and preaching.
- He was born into nobility but gave up all wealth to become a Dominican Friar.
- The sun is his symbol because, "he both brings the light of learning into the minds of men and fires their hearts and wills with the virtues." –Pope Pius XI
- Quill pen for writing
- He was an author, and his most famous book is called "Summa Theologica."
- It is said that he had the ability to levitate (float) while praying.
- "There is nothing on this earth more to be prized than true friendship." –St. Thomas
- Thomas was a student of scientist, St. Albert the Great, who was known as "teacher of everything there is to know."

St. John Bosco
Birth: August 16, 1815 in Becchi, Piedmont, Italy
Death: January 31, 1888 in Turin, Italy
Canonization: April 1, 1934 by Pope Pius XI

John was raised by his devout mother who instilled the faith in him at a very young age. His father died when John was 2 years old, causing financial struggles for the family. Instead of attending school regularly, John had to work on the family farm with his older brothers.

Patron saint of schoolchildren, youth, and publishers

When John was 9 years old, he had a spiritual dream that inspired him to help young people, especially underprivileged and troubled boys, to know Jesus and live virtuous lives. John desired to become a holy priest dedicated to ministering to the youth.

He was a brilliant preacher and writer and published books and newsletters.

He was called "Don Bosco," which in Italy means "Father Bosco."

Despite the hardships at home, John's mother was very supportive of his endeavors and encouraged him to attend a school away from home where he could study for the priesthood.

As a young boy, John would entertain his peers with juggling and acrobatics. Instead of charging an entrance fee, he requested acts of piety such as praying a Hail Mary or doing a good deed.

He founded an Oratory, an all-boys boarding school that focused on the spiritual well-being and education of disadvantaged boys, many whom he found homeless on the streets of Turin.

His signature style was the black cassock.

Whenever John was in danger, a gray dog would mysteriously appear to protect him. He named the dog "Grigio," which means "grey."

"It's easy to be a Saint. I want to give you the formula for sanctity: first, be happy; second, study and pray; third, do good to everyone." –St. John Bosco

He founded the Salesian Order named after one of his favorite saints, St. Francis de Sales.

Thanks to his spiritual guidance he led many to become Saints, including his student St. Dominic Savio!

John was known to experience very real and prophetic spiritual dreams that guided his actions and teachings throughout life.

ST. JOHN BOSCO Feast Day January 31

4

St. Blaise
Birth: in the 3rd Century A.D.
Death: in the year 316 A.D. in Sebastea, Armenia

Blaise was a bishop who ministered to the spiritual and physical needs of his people. He lived during a time when the Roman Empire was persecuting Christians. After receiving a message from God that he should flee to avoid the persecutions, Blaise retreated to the mountains where he lived among wild animals and cured the sick. He eventually was found, and while being taken away, enountered a boy who was choking on a fish bone. Blaise healed him and for that reason he is patron of those with throat ailments.

Protector of wild animals and patron saint of those suffering from illnesses of the throat

Blaise talked a wolf into releasing a pig that belonged to a poor woman. In thanksgiving, the woman brought Blaise food and candles to light his cell after he was captured.

He was a Christian martyr who refused to worship pagan idols.

During the blessing of throats, given on Blaise's feast day, the priest holds two crossed and unlit candles against each person's throat while saying the blessing prayer.

In San Carlo Church in Rome, some of his relics are stored. They are only exposed during the blessing on his feast day. In Dubrovnik, many of his relics are presevered, including his throat!

The blessing prayer of St. Blaise:
"Through the intercession of St. Blaise, bishop and martyr, may God deliver you from all ailments of the throat and from every other illness. In the name of the Father, and of the Son and of the Holy Spirit. Amen."

It is thought that Blaise was a doctor before becoming a priest and bishop.

The blessing of St. Blaise is a popular tradition, particularly in the U.S., Germany, Croatia and Italy.

ST. BLAISE
Feast Day February 3

ST. KATHARINE DREXEL
Feast Day March 3

St. Katharine
Birth: November 26, 1858, in Philadelphia, Pennsylvania
Death: March 3, 1955, in Bensalem Township, Pennsylvania
Canonized: October 1, 2000 by St. Pope John Paul II

Katharine lived during a time when African Americans and Native Americans were mistreated because of their race. She had a deep concern for their physical and spiritual well-being and did whatever she could to help them.

Patron saint of philanthropy and racial justice

St. Francis Cabrini mentored her.

Nickname: "Kate"

She had a private meeting with Pope Leo XIII asking him to send missionaries to the Native Americans. To her surprise, the pope told Katharine to become one!

Katharine's parents were wealthy and helped the less fortunate by making donations to charities. This taught Katharine to be generous at an early age. But Katharine wanted to do more than help people with their physical needs. She wanted to help take care of their souls too. When she grew up, she founded a religious order, Sisters of the Blessed Sacrament, whose focus is prayer and ministry to African and Native American people.

She is often pictured wearing glasses.

She is the second U.S. saint to be canonized

She founded missions and schools for African and Native Americans in over fifteen states.

Her crucifix was made of ebony.

She wore a black religious habit.

"My sweetest joy is to be in the presence of Jesus in the holy Sacrament."
–St. Katharine

She is buried at the National Shrine of St. Katharine Drexel, in Bensalem, Pennsylvania.

She spent the last few years of her life quietly dedicated to Eucharistic Adoration.

She founded Xavier University in New Orleans, Louisiana.

St. Dominic Savio

Birth: April 2, 1842 in Riva, Italy
Death: March 9, 1857 in Turin, Italy
Canonization: June 12, 1954 by Pope Pius XII

Dominic Savio was raised in a small village by his Catholic parents who knew from a young age that he was a very special child. At 4 years old, Dominic knew his prayers by heart, and by age 5, he was an altar server. Since he wanted to be a priest, he attended the Oratory school of Fr. John Bosco. Dominic was a joyful student who had many friends. He was a good role model, encouraging his peers to always make good choices, to avoid sin and to pray and receive the Sacraments often. Dominic died of tuberculosis shortly before turning 15.

Patron saint of the falsely accused, choir boys, altar servers and the youth

Dominic started a club at his school that focused on growing closer to the Blessed Mother.

Dominic had a special gift of knowledge. One night he awoke Fr. Bosco and urged him to rush to a specific address. Upon arriving, the saintly priest found a very ill man begging for Confession and Last Rites.

He was determined to be a saint after hearing a sermon that expressed:
*God wills that each person should become a saint.
*It is easy to become a saint.
*There is a great reward in heaven for those who try to become saints.

One day, without receiving any news from his family, he asked to go home for the day. When he arrived, his pregnant mother was experiencing severe pain in labor. He hugged and kissed her, placed a green scapular around her, and left. The pain went away and his mother safely delivered his baby sister, Catherine.

He died peacefully with a smile on his face saying "Oh, what wonderful things I see!" as he raised his hands in the air towards heaven.

When two of his friends were about to fight, Dominic stood before them, holding a crucifix. Instead of fighting, the boys made peace and went to confession.

St. John Bosco wrote a biography on his life called, "The Life of St. Dominic Savio."

The four promises he made on the day of his First Holy Communion were:
1. To go to confession often and attend daily Mass.
2. Keep holy Sundays and special feast days.
3. His best friends would be Jesus and Mary.
4. Death rather than sin.

"Ask Jesus to make you a saint."
–St. Dominic Savio

"I am not capable of doing big things, but I want to do everything, even the smallest things, for the greater glory of God." – St. Dominic Savio

ST. DOMINIC SAVIO
Feast Day March 9

St. Patrick

Birth: 387, in Kilpatrick, Scotland
Death: March 17, 461 in Saul, Downpatrick, Ireland

ST. PATRICK — *Feast Day March 17*

Patron saint of Ireland

Patrick was the first person to bring the Gospel message to Ireland. He converted and baptized many people, including kings and entire kingdoms!

Bishop's mitre

He was the first bishop of Ireland.

Bishop's crozier

Many believe that Ireland has no native snakes thanks to the miracle performed by Patrick. It is said that while he was making a 40-day fast on top of a hill, snakes started to attack him. He commanded them to fall into the sea, and they did!

When he was a teenager, Patrick was taken captive from his native Scotland to Ireland and became a slave, working in the fields as a shepherd. At that time, Ireland was a pagan country. During his captivity, Patrick grew stronger in his faith. He would pray to God constantly throughout the day. When Patrick was about 20 years old, he had a dream that God told him to go to the sea, and a boat would be waiting to take him to freedom. He walked 200 miles to the sea and there was indeed a boat, which took him safely home to his family.

Patrick kept a prayer journal while he was a slave in Ireland.

"Christ with me,
Christ before me,
Christ behind me,
Christ in me,
Christ beneath me,
Christ above me..."
–St. Patrick

Patrick was ordained a priest by St. Germanus!

Patrick taught the mystery of the Holy Trinity, three persons in one God, through the symbol of the Shamrock, which has three heart shaped leaves in one plant.

After becoming a priest, Patrick felt called to return to Ireland. He had a longing to bring Christ to the Irish. When Patrick was elected a Bishop, he was given the opportunity to minister there.

ST. FRANCIS OF PAOLA
Feast Day April 2

St. Francis of Paola
Birth: March 27, 1416 in Calabria, Italy
Death: April 2, 1507 in Plessis, France
Canonized: 1519 by Pope Leo X

Before Francis was born, his parents prayed through the intercession of St. Francis of Assisi to have a child, promising to name him after the saint. Then again, when Francis became sick as a baby, they petitioned his patron, promising they would educate him under the Franciscan Order and allow him to become a friar if it were God's will. As a young boy, he did desire to live according to the Rule of St. Francis of Assisi.

Patron saint of sailors, mariners and naval officers

"Put aside hatred and hostility...Be lovers of peace."
–St. Francis of Paola

Francis was sent to France to minister to King Louis the XI. He helped the king come back to God shortly before the king died. He also guided the king in restoring peace between France and Spain.

Francis was capable of numerous miracles and could predict the future.

His nickname is "Fire Handler" for performing a miracle with fire.

Francis needed to go to Sicily, an island off of Italy. He asked a sailor to take him there, but because Francis took the vow of poverty, he had no money to offer. So the sailor refused. Francis took off his cloak, tied it to his cane and sailed on it to Sicily. That is why he is the patron saint of sailors.

Francis founded an order called the Minims, which in Latin means "the least." They wear the Franciscan habit, follow the same Rule and take the same vows but with an additional one of fasting.

He taught the importance of being kind and humble and doing penance.

Once, the friars working in the monastery complained that they had to walk too far to collect water. So Francis tapped his cane on a rock, and fresh water sprung from it.

Praying the rosary was an important part of his day.

ST. GEMMA GALGANI
Feast Day April 11

St. Gemma
Birth: March 12, 1878 in Camigliano, Lucca, Italy
Death: April 11, 1903 on Holy Saturday, in Lucca, Italy
Canonization: May 2, 1940 by Pope Pius XII.

St. Gemma was a natural beauty. To practice the virtue of modesty, she chose to always dress plainly in black. She even stopped wearing jewelry once she realized it drew attention to her. This practice humbled her and helped free her from the desire of vanity.

Nickname: "The Gem of Christ"

Patron saint of students, pharmacists, loss of parents, and those who suffer from head and back pain.

She was a gifted student in math, music, religion and French.

She wanted to be a Passionist nun, but her health would not permit it. Still, she remained close to the order and her tomb and relics can be venerated at their monastery in Lucca.

She had a special devotion to St. Gabriel of the Sorrowful Mother. Gemma suffered from a very serious illness, but was miraculously cured after he appeared to her in a vision.

She found joy in suffering and making sacrifices. She embraced the cross daily.

She was given the rare and special gift of the wounds of Christ, called the Stigmata, which would come to her on Thursdays and go away by Friday or Saturday morning.

Gemma had such a close relationship to her guardian angel that the two had conversations. Her guardian angel was known to deliver Gemma's letters to her spiritual director who lived in another town!

From a young age, Gemma had a deep prayer life and love for the Eucharist. Every morning she would wake up and walk to Mass. She would not speak to anyone until after she had received Jesus in Communion.

"I say 'Jesus, Your will and not mine.' At last, I am convinced that only God can make me happy, and in Him I have placed all my hope..." –St Gemma

ST. MARK
Feast Day April 25

St. Mark

Birth: First Century Ayrene, North Africa (present day Libya)
Death: 68 A.D. in Alexandria (present day Egypt)

Mark was born a Jew and spoke Hebrew. He converted to Christianity after the Resurrection. It is believed the he actually never met Jesus but met Peter and became a disciple through him. He was in Rome when Peter was Pope. Not only was he Peter's disciple, he was also his interpreter. He wrote the Gospel according to what Peter told him. Peter sent him to be a missionary in Africa and anointed him the first Bishop of Alexandria (present day Egypt).

Patron saint of notaries, Venice and Egypt

He writes of Jesus' love for children and how He blessed them and said, "Let the children come to me...for the kingdom of God belongs to such as these..." (Mark 10:13-16)

Thanks to Mark's mission the Christian faith was brought to Egypt.

He wrote one of the four Gospels!

His mother's house was a meeting place for the early Christians. (Acts 12:12)

He was a friend of Sts. Paul and Barnabas. In fact it is thought that St. Barnabas was his cousin.

He went on a mission with Paul and Barnabas to the Island of Cyprus.

Unbelievers in Alexandria thought the miracles that Mark performed in his life were magic, so they seized him while he was celebrating Mass. He died a Christian martyr. His last words were of thanksgiving and praise to God.

Mark wrote the second Gospel most likely when he was living in Rome in about the year 60 A.D.

His tomb and relics are in the Basilica San Marco in Venice, Italy.

He wrote the Gospel in Greek for the Gentile converts to understand.

Mark's Gospel reveals how Jesus came to save humanity by serving and sacrificing his life for us. He describes Jesus as a man of action who ministered to the Galileans.

11

OUR LADY OF FATIMA
Feast Day May 13

Our Lady of Fatima
Place of Apparition: Fatima, Portugal

Patroness of all of humanity, world peace and Portugal

The Blessed Mother Mary appeared above an oak tree to the "children of Fatima" – Lucia, Francisco and Jacinta – while they were pasturing their sheep. She first appeared on May 13, 1917. She asked the children to return to that place on the 13th of each month for six consecutive months and then she would bring a miracle. During her meetings she told the children three secrets about the future that, decades later, actually occurred. On the last meeting, October 13, 1917, in the middle of a rainy day, the clouds cleared and the sun spun in the sky. "The Miracle of the Sun" was witnessed by the children and many curious townspeople.

When Pope Francis was elected, he consecrated his entire papacy to Our Lady of Fatima.

"My Immaculate Heart will be your refuge and the way that will lead you to God." –Our Lady of Fatima

Prior to her appearance, an Angel of Peace appeared to the children and gave them this prayer to recite daily: "My God, I believe, I adore, I hope, and I love you. I ask pardon for those who do not believe, do not adore, do not hope and do not love you."

Pope Benedict XVI visited the shrine of Our Lady of Fatima on her feast day in 2010 and reflected that Mary inspired the shepherd children to fall in love with Jesus by teaching them "a deep knowledge of the Love of the Blessed Trinity…"

St. John Paul II had a great devotion to her and attributed his life being saved by her "invisible hand" in 1981 when a bullet almost pierced his heart. That bullet is now in the crown of the original statue of Our Lady of Fatima as a reminder of her love and intercession for all mankind.

During his papacy, St. John Paul II renewed the consecration of the entire human race to the Immaculate Heart of Mary.

She asked the children to pray the rosary daily for the conversion of sinners and world peace.

She appeared in a white dress "more brilliant than the sun, shedding rays of light…" –Lucia Dos Santos

She referred to herself as Our Lady of the Rosary.

A chapel is built over the place where she appeared and is a major pilgrimage spot.

St. Dymphna
Birth: 7th Century in Ireland
Death: On May 15th between the years 620-640 in Geel, Belgium

ST. DYMPHNA — Feast Day May 15

Dymphna was raised in Ireland by her mother and father, but her Christian mother died when she was only 14 years old. This caused her father, who was a pagan king, to become so depressed, he ended up suffering from a mental disorder and doing bad things. But Dymphna refused to let him talk her into sinning. She stood firm in her faith, and she was willing to give her life for her strong moral beliefs.

Patron saint of people afflicted with epilepsy, mental illness, depression, anxiety, emotional and neurological disorders

Her relics in Geel, Belgium have been known to cure insanity and epilepsy.

Nickname: "Lily of Fire" because of her purity and passionate love for Jesus.

After Dymphna gave her life for the faith, her body was buried in a cave. Years later, the people of Geel wanted to give her a proper burial. When they arrived at the cave, to their surprise, they found a tomb made of beautiful, pure white stone. It was as if angels had made it. On her chest lay a red tile identifying her. It read, "Here lies the holy virgin and martyr Dymphna."

She is a model and intercessor for the defense of purity.

Red tile on the Bible representing a mysterious marker that indentified her body years after her death.

Lily for purity

Bible with shamrock representing the Holy Trinity

We can pray for her intercession to help us in stressful moments or whenever we are worried.

She is wearing an Irish dress because she was a royal princess in Ireland.

She died a martyr at the age of 15.

St. Joan of Arc

Birth: January 6, 1412 in France
Death: May 30, 1431 in Normandy, under English Rule, now part of France.
Canonized: May 16, 1920 by Pope Benedict XV

ST. JOAN OF ARC Feast Day May 30

Joan lived during a time when France was being overtaken by England. At 13 years old, she started seeing visions of Sts. Michael, Catherine, and Margaret, telling her to go to King Charles VII and help him reclaim the French Kingdom. Due to her young age and her gender, it was difficult for her to convince the male-only military that she knew the winning strategy. With the king's support, the military finally gave in, and with God on her side, Joan, at 17 years old, led a troop of soldiers to recapture the cities of Orleans and Troyes, a key conquest for the French during the Hundred Years War. Her leadership and courage re-established the Catholic Faith in France.

Patron saint of France and soldiers

She is known as the heroine of France!

Joan was influential in spreading the Catholic faith in France.

"I would rather die than do something which I know to be a sin, or to be against God's will."
– St. Joan of Arc

She loved praying, going to Church, and helping the sick and the poor.

She hid her long hair and disguised herself as a male soldier.

The banner she carried in battle bore the words, "Jesus Maria," a figure of God the Father, and two kneeling angels presenting Him a fleur-de-lis, which is a lily.

The Fleur-de-lis is the royal emblem of France. The flag represents victory.

She is wearing military armor and holding a sword for battle.

When she was captured by the enemy, she was called a heretic for sharing the messages she recieved from heaven. She was burned at the stake for defending the Faith.

The saints who spoke to her told her that she would not live long, yet she still followed God's will!

Fire-colored dress under her armor is a symbol of how she was martyrd.

Anthony was a Franciscan priest during the time that St. Francis was alive. Anthony desired to be a missionary in Africa, however, after a severe storm, the boat he was traveling on landed in Italy. He subsequently became a missionary in Italy, and was assigned to the city of Padua.

St. Anthony
Birth: 1195 A.D. in Lisbon, Portugal
Death: June 13, 1231, in Padua, Italy
Canonization: May 30, 1232 by Pope Gregory IX

Patron saint of lost and stolen articles, Portugal, and Padua, Italy

Anthony was known to be a gifted preacher, teacher and writer. He was declared a Doctor of the Church and is known as "Evangelical Doctor" because of his dynamic yet simple ways of teaching the faith.

Semi-bald haircut in the shape of a halo. Called a "tonsure," this hairstyle worn by some monks is a form of mortification, a way to give up what we want and suffer for Jesus.

After preaching about Jesus to a group of unbelievers who paid him no attention, Anthony remarked that fish would be better listeners. His statement turned out to be true when a multitude of fish swam to the shore to hear his preaching.

A brown habit represents a Franciscan Friar.

A close friend of Anthony's once saw a bright light coming from his room. When the friend peeked in, he saw Anthony holding and talking to baby Jesus.

He could quote scripture by heart.

Anthony lost a very important psalm book. After he prayed to find the book, the novice who stole it and ran away from the Friary not only returned the book but gave his heart back to the Lord.

"Attribute to God every good that you have received." –St. Anthony

ST. ANTHONY OF PADUA
Feast Day June 13

ST. MARIA GORETTI
Feast Day July 6

St. Maria Goretti
Birth: October 16, 1890 in Corinaldo, Italy
Death: July 6, 1902 in Nettuno, Italy
Canonized: June 24, 1950 by Pope Pius XII

Maria is known for her beauty, courage, and love for Jesus. She died a virgin and martyr at the age of 11. Her story is sad but glorious. Throughout her life, Maria kept close to her heart the words her mother told her: "You must never commit sin, at any cost."

Patron saint of the youth, young women, purity and victims of rape

When Maria was 11 years old, a teen boy she knew tried to make her sin. She refused, telling him, "No! It is a sin! God does not want it." Even though he fatally wounded her, she forgave him before she died.

Her family and friends called her "Marietta."

While on her deathbed, Maria was asked if she forgave her attacker. She said, "Yes, I forgive him and want him to be in Paradise with me some day."

What we can learn from Maria Goretti:
*To be courageous for our faith and resist peer pressure.
*To pray for the grace of purity and chastity.
*To forgive and pray for those who hurt us.

Maria's intercession from heaven led to the conversion of the young man who hurt her. In his dream, Alessandro saw Maria in a garden where she spoke to him and presented him with white lilies. After the dream, he repented, asked Maria's mother to forgive him and lived a life for Jesus. He and Maria's mother were present at Maria's canonization!

Lilies symbolize her purity.

Palm branches show she was a martyr.

Her body is at Our Lady of Mercy in Nettuno, Italy.

ST. BENEDICT
Feast Day July 11

St. Benedict
Birth: 480 A.D. in Nursia, Italy
Death: 547 while standing in prayer to God in Monte Cassino, Italy

Benedict is the father of monasticism, a religious way of life dedicated to prayer and the works of God. The "Rule of St. Benedict" is instructions on religious life which is still used today in the Church after 15 centuries. It consists of Liturgical prayer, study, manual labor, and living together in community under a common father, an "abbot."

Patron saint of Europe, school children, a happy death and those suffering from kidney disease and poisoning.

He went to the mountains to live as a hermit, alone in deep solitude and prayer. This time with God helped shape his interior life.

Four to six hours of his day were set aside for Sacred reading.

Benedict compiled and recommended a prayer that was to be chanted at specific hours of the day; which became the prayer of the Church called the Divine Office.

His monastery was called Monte Cassino. It marked the beginning of the Church's monastic system.

He is the founder of the Benedictine Order.

Once someone who wanted to harm him gave him a drink that would make him sick. But Benedict made the sign of the cross over it and the cup shattered so he could not drink it.

The St. Benedict Medal is a Christian sacramental with symbols and words related to Benedict's life. It is one of the oldest and most honored medals used by Christians. It is considered a "devil chasing medal."

The St. Benedict Cross is used by priests during exorcism.

Benedict was very wise, and people came to him to learn how to be holy. He taught them to pray and work hard and always be humble. He and his monks helped teach people to read, write, farm and train for various trade jobs.

"Put Christ before all else."
–the Rule of St. Benedict

His sister Scholastica is also a Saint!

ST. VERONICA
Feast Day July 12

St. Veronica
Birth: Around the time of Jesus
Death: First Century

Veronica is known as the woman of Jerusalem who used her veil to wipe the sweat and blood from Jesus' face while he was carrying the cross to Golgotha. She did this out of pity and love for him. An imprint of Jesus' face, exactly as it was when it was wiped, appeared on her veil.

Patron saint of photographers and laundry workers

We remember her act of compassion during the the Sixth Station of the Cross: "Veronica Wipes the Face of Jesus."

She boldly stepped out from the crowd to provide some reprieve to our Lord as he was struggling under the weight of the cross.

Her face is painted to express sorrow and compassion for our suffering Lord.

In Latin her name means "true image."

The image of Jesus' face miraculously appeared on her veil.

Her feast day is known as the "Holy Face of Jesus."

The veil is stored in a small chapel in St. Peter's Basilica, Rome, and is brought out on the fifth Sunday of Lent for all present to receive a blessing.

What we can learn from Veronica:
*To be courageous and compassionate to those in need.
*To step out of our comfort to help others.

ST. KATERI TEKAKWITHA
Feast Day July 14

St. Kateri
Birth: 1656 in Ossernenon (modern day Auriesville), New York
Death: April 17, 1680 in Quebec, Canada
Canonized: 2012 by Pope St. John Paul II

Kateri was the daughter of a Mohawk chief. Her mother was a Christian convert. She was left an orphan at the age of 4 after a small pox epidemic. She was adopted by her aunt and uncle. Kateri became Catholic as a teenager and was baptized on Easter Sunday. As a Christian, she endured hostility from her tribe. She moved to a Christian colony in Canada where she was devoted to prayer and serving the sick and elderly.

Patron saint of the environment, ecology, people ridiculed for their piety and Native Americans

She was known for having a gentle and kind spirit and a good sense of humor.

She was considered an outcast in her tribe for being a Christian. But she did not let that stop her from loving and living for Jesus.

When family and friends were mean to her for being a Christian, she grew closer to the Lord, knowing he, too, was once persecuted.

Kateri is derived from the name Katherine.

Nickname: "Lily of the Mohawks"

Jesuit missionaries baptized her and guided her in her spiritual growth.

An illness she had at 4 years old left her with scars on her face and bad vision.

She is the first Native American saint.

She was named Tekakwitha by her uncle because it means "she who bumps into things," referring to her poor eyesight.

Her dress is made of natural leather colors and she holds a wood-colored cross to represent her Native American heritage.

She enjoyed going on rosary walks where she would meditate on each mystery.

She became ill and died at the age of 24.

ST. MARY MAGDALENE
Feast Day July 22

St. Mary Magdalene
She was a Jew (later baptized a Christian) from the town of Magdale in Northern Galilee.

Mary Magdalene is thought to be the sinful woman who showed sorrow for her sins by weeping at the feet of Jesus, drying them with her hair and anointing them with expensive perfume. Moved by her love and humility, Jesus said to her, "Your sins are forgiven…Your faith has saved you; go in peace."

Patron of contemplative life, converts, penitent sinners, hairstylists, those ridiculed for their piety, and women

After Mary's conversion, she was a faithful follower of Jesus and spent her life ministering to Him and His disciples.

Jesus freed Mary Magdalene from the grasp of seven demons. (Mark 16:9)

Nickname: Apostle to the Apostles (given to her by St. Gregory the Great)

Mary Magdalene went to the tomb of Jesus to anoint His body with spices, as was the custom at that time. She found the tomb empty! An angel told her the Good News that Jesus had been raised and asked her to take the message to His disciples.

She was one of the three faithful women that stood at the cross of Jesus when he died. (John 19:25)

She wiped the feet of Jesus with her long hair.

She is known as the "penitent" or the "repentant sinner."

Red symbolizes sin and redemption–God's mercy.

Mary Magdalene was the first person to learn that Jesus had risen from the dead. She was weeping outside his empty tomb and thought he was the gardener until Jesus called her by name, "Mary!" Then she immediately recognized the Lord.

A tall jar representing the perfume and spices for annointing Jesus

"I have seen the Lord!"
–St. Mary Magdalene
(John 20:18)

What we can learn from Mary Magdalene:
*Jesus calls us by name.
*We often don't recognize the voice of God.
*Repentance for sin brings us closer to Jesus.

ST. JAMES THE GREATER
Feast Day July 25

St. James
Birth: 1st Century in Galilee
Death: 44 A.D. in Judea (Acts 12:2)
He died 14 years after Jesus' death and resurrection

James was fishing with his brother, father and friends, Peter and Andrew, when Jesus called him. James dropped everything he was doing to follow Jesus, becoming one of His twelve apostles.
(Mark 13:3)

Patron saint of pilgrims, laborers, veternarians, equestrians and Spain

Jesus called James and John "Sons of Thunder" perhaps for their passion and temper. Jesus even scolded James for being unforgiving and prideful when dealing with people. But James was faithful to Jesus to the end, trying his hardest to do what would please the Lord, and so became a saint.

James was one of the first Christian martyrs.
(Acts 12:1)

Over hundreds of years, millions of people have walked to his tomb in Compostela, Spain, on a famous pilgrimage known as "The Way of St. James." Even St. Francis walked the hundred of miles on "The Way," which people still travel today on foot, stopping at Holy sites and seeking God's will for their lives.

Jesus gave James and his apostles authority to heal the people, cast out demons and preach the Good News.

St. James was the apostle who brought Christianity to Spain.

James is often depicted with a scallop shell. The shell was used to baptize new Christians.

James' parents and brother are each mentioned in the Gospels. His father was Zebedee, his younger brother was the apostle John, and his mother Salome was present at the foot of the cross.

James, was one of the three disciples (along with John and Peter) to:
* Witnesss Jesus bring back to life the daughter of Jairus.
* See the Transfiguration of Jesus.
* Pray in the Garden of Gethsemane with Jesus after the Last Supper.

He is called James "the Greater" because there was another apostle named James who was younger.

ST. CHRISTOPHER
Feast Day July 25

St. Christopher

Birth: Unknown, but it is believed he lived during the 3rd Century in what is now present day Turkey

Death: It is believed he died a martyr around the year 251 A.D. in what is now present day Turkey

Stories based on Christopher's life have been passed down over the centuries, though written historical records are sparse. He is described as a very tall and strong man. He was a convert to the Christian faith and desired to serve the Lord by helping others. Where he lived, there was a raging river without a bridge that people had to cross often. Since travelers could easily be swept away in the river, Christopher decided to use his strength and serve as a "human ferry". He helped the travelers cross by carrying them.

Patron saint of travelers, surfers, mariners, storms and epilepsy

His name means "Christ-bearer"

The most famous story about St. Christopher tells us that, while carrying a child across the river, the child became so heavy, Christopher thought they would both fall and be swept away. When Christopher questioned the child about his heaviness, the child told him he was Jesus and that Christopher was carrying Him who was holding the whole world and the weight of the world's sins.

Statues and images of St. Christopher with the inscription, "Whoever shall behold the image of St. Christopher shall not faint or fall on that day," can be viewed in a variety of ancient Churches throughout Europe and the East.

Christopher carried the Christ Child, who had the weight of the whole world on his shoulders.

It is said that, once on the other side of the river, the Christ Child requested Christopher push his walking staff into the ground and He miraculously turned it into a fruit-bearing tree.

It was a popular tradition in the early centuries to erect a statue of St. Christopher at the entrance to a bridge as a symbol of protection.

ST. IGNATUS OF LOYOLA
Feast Day July 31

St. Ignatius
Birth: October 23, 1491 in Loyola, Spain
Death: July 31, 1556 in Rome, Italy
Canonization: 1622 by Pope Gregory XV

Ignatius, born into nobility, lived during the time of kingdoms and battles. He aspired to be a valiant soldier, however a serious leg wound required him to take time away from the battlefield to rest in bed and heal. Television and computers were not yet invented, so to keep him entertained he requested books. He was given the holy Bible and stories on the lives of saints. Although Ignatius was baptized Catholic, he was not religious so these were not the books he was expecting, but given no other option, he read them. This period of recovery led him to his conversion to Christ. He decided that he would no longer be a soldier for his country, but a solider for Christ, and he decided to become a priest.

Patron saint of all Spiritual retreats, educators, education, soldiers, Jesuits, and Basque Country, Spain

Ignatius studied at the university in Paris. There he became friends with Sts. Francis Xavier and Peter Faber.

His name in Spanish is "Ignacio" and his nickname was "Iñigo"

He was the main founder of the relgious order, the Society of Jesus, also known as the Jesuits.

He is famous for writing the "Spiritual Exercises," a guide for deepening one's prayer life.

Pope Francis is a Jesuit!

Ignatius admired the life of St. Francis of Assisi and decided that his order would take the same three vows that Franciscans take: Poverty, Chastity and Obedience as well as a fourth vow of Absolute Obedience to the Pope.

His motto was "Ad maiorem Dei gloriam" (AMDG), which in Latin means, "For the greater glory of God!"

He was the youngest of 13 children!

"Go forth, and set the world on fire." –St. Ignatius

23

ST. JOHN VIANNEY
Feast Day August 4

St. John Vianney
Birth: May 8, 1786, in Dardilly, France
Death: August 4, 1859, in Ars-sur-Formans
Canonized: 1925 by Pope Pius XI

John Vianney lived through the French Revolution, which lasted from 1789 to 1799. During that time, Catholics had to practice their faith in secret, or they could be arrested and killed. John's family would go to secret places to attend Mass. He made his First Communion in a room with covered windows so as not to draw attention from the outside. In his eyes, priests were heroes because they risked their lives to bring Jesus to the people.

Patron saint of priests

He would spend up to sixteen hours a day hearing confessions!

John had a special devotion to St. Philomena. When he fell gravely ill, he sought her intercession. After he was miraculously healed, he promised to celebrate one hundred Masses in thanksgiving in the chapel he had named after her.

Although he was drafted by Napoleon's army twice, he never had to go to war. The first time, he was in the hospital for an illness, and the second time, he was left behind after stopping in a church to pray.

His body is incorrupt! He lays as if sleeping above the main altar in the Basilica in Ars, France.

He was well-known as a phenomenal spiritual director and confessor. People came to see him from all over the world, to get advice and confess their sins.

He was baptized the same day that he was born!

The bishop and 300 priests presided at his funeral with over 6000 people in attendance!

In school he struggled to learn Latin and had to hire a tutor.

His advice on following Christ: "Belong wholly to God."

His full name in French is Jean-Baptise-Marie Vianney.

Nickname: Cure de Ars, which in French means "Priest of Ars"

"We are each of us like a small mirror in which God searches for His reflection."
–Saint John Vianney

St. Monica

Birth: 332 A.D., Tagaste, Northern Africa (Algeria)
Death: 387 A.D., Ostia, Italy

Monica had a difficult home life because her husband was a pagan and had a bad temper. Her mother-in-law and son Augustine also did not believe in God. Monica prayed fervently for their conversions and after years of prayer all three became Christians!

Monica is an example of never losing hope in God, keeping firm in the faith and persevering in prayer.

Patron saint of wives, mothers, difficult marriages, and victims of abuse

She was instrumental in bringing three generations of family to the Christian Faith.

In the Basilica of Sant'Agostino in Rome there is a special side chapel dedicated to Monica and her selpuchre (tomb) where people can visit and pray.

She would beg priests and bishops to pray for the conversion of her son, Augustine. One bishop told her "it is not possible that a son of so many tears should perish."

She holds a staff because she came from a wealthy family and married into nobility.

Tears for the many tears she wept for her son.

She had three children: two boys and a girl, Augustine, Navigius and Perpetua

Monica's husband would not let her baptize their children as babies, but Monica still taught her children Jesus' love by reading to them from the Bible. Eventually, all three of her children were baptized Christians.

She had a very loving relationship with her children, despite their differences.

"Nothing is far from God."
–St Monica

After 17 years of tears and prayers, her son converted and was baptized. His changed life in Christ was so significant that he even became a bishop and a canonized Saint!

ST. MONICA Feast Day August 27

Bl. Mother Teresa

Birth: August 26, 1910 in Skopje, Macedonia (present day Albania)
Death: September 5, 1997 in Calcutta, India
Beatification: October 19, 2003 by Pope John Paul II

Mother Teresa is a modern-day saint. As a sister, she taught at a high school in Calcutta, India, until an illness required her to stop teaching and rest. During her recovery she felt a strong call from God to work and live among the poor in the slums of Calcutta.

Mother Teresa learned basic nursing skills and began taking care of "the poorest of the poor:" sick homeless men, women and children whom even hospitals refused to help. She rented rooms to care for them, which eventually led to her opening the "Home for the Dying." Other women joined Teresa on her mission to care for the poor, forgotten, unwanted people in Calcutta, and she established a religious order called the Missionaries of Charity.

BLESSED MOTHER TERESA — Feast Day September 5

Her birth name was Agnes. When she became a sister, she chose the name Teresa to honor St. Therese of Lisieux

As a teenager, she attended a youth group led by Jesuits. This introduced her to missions and inspired her desire to be a missionary.

She was a true follower of the Gospel – a woman of love, self-sacrifice, courage, mercy and peace.

When she won the Nobel Peace Prize in 1979, she requested that the money that would have been used for a ceremonial banquet be sent to the poor in Calcutta.

Her trademark dress is a white sari with blue

St. Pope John Paul II was her friend!

Mother Teresa's zeal for those in need made an impact in every corner of the world.

She had a compassionate heart for every single person that she met whether rich or poor, healthy or sick, young or old, she loved them all.

She spoke on the dignity of every person, from conception to natural death. She did not fear criticism or rejection and was outspoken on all Christian beliefs, yet she was a woman of peace.

"Keep the joy of loving God in your heart and share this joy with all you meet especially your family. Be holy.
—Mother Teresa

St. Padre Pio

Birth: May 25, 1887, Pietrelcina, Italy
Death: September 23, 1968, San Giovanni Rotondo, Italy
Canonization: June 16, 2002 by Pope John Paul II

ST. PIO OF PIETRELCINA
Feast Day September 23

Pio was a priest of the Capuchin Order of the Friars Minor. He was ordained at 23 years old. He was a very humble man who was known to spend the whole day hearing confessions, after he celebrated the Holy Mass, which was the highlight of his day. God gave Pio many gifts that attracted thousands and allowed him to bring people closer to the Lord.

He could read hearts, convert souls to Christ by just his presence or words, understand and speak in languages he never studied, predict the future, discern Spirits, heal the sick, perform miracles and bilocate.

Patron saint of the youth and civil defense volunteers

He suffered from poor health his whole life, but that did not stop him as he offered his sufferings to God as a sacrifice for the conversion of souls.

He is the first priest in the history of the Church to have the stigmata (the wounds of Christ).

He was like a modern day super hero! He could go without sleep and nourishment beyond man's natural powers. This helped him spend more time ministering to God's people.

People have reported miracles received through the gloves he wore over his wounds.

He always wrote back to all of his spiritual children who wrote letters to him.

What we can learn from St. Padre Pio:
*To pray always!
*To go to confession and Mass frequently.
*To seek God's will in our life each day.

Since he was a young boy he could see and chat with his guardian angel, Jesus and Mary and he did not realize this special grace because he thought everyone could.

"Pray, hope and don't worry."
–St. Pio

27

ST. GABRIEL THE ARCHANGEL
Feast Day September 29

St. Gabriel

In Hebrew, the name Gabriel means "man of God" or "strength of God." He appears by name in both the Old and New Testament.

Patron saint of messengers, communication workers and postal workers.

Archangel Gabriel appeared to Mary to tell her that she would bear a son, conceived by the Holy Spirit, and He would be called Jesus, the Son of the Most High, Savior of the World. Gabriel had also appeared to Zechariah to announce that his aging wife, Elizabeth, was pregnant with a son who was to be named John. That baby was John the Baptist, Jesus' cousin, whose mission was to prepare the way for Jesus. You can read all about it in the first chapter of Luke.

It is thought that Gabriel may have been the unnamed angel who appears throughout the New Testament giving messages of wisdom, strength and hope to St. Joseph (Matthew 1:20-24), the Shepherds of the Nativity (Luke 2:9-14), Jesus (Luke 22:43), and Mary Magdalene at the empty tomb (Mark 16:5-7).

St. Gabriel is known as a messenger from God.

The beginning of the Hail Mary prayer comes from the greeting of Gabriel to Mary, "Hail, favored one! The Lord is with you." (Luke 1:28)

In the Old Testament angel Gabriel appears to Daniel as a man and interprets a prophetic vision for Daniel.

The scepter represents authority

Lilies represent purity

He is holding a mirror, made of a stone called "jasper." The mirror is thought to represent the wisdom of God as well as purity. It is marked with an "X," the first initial in the Greek word, Χριστός, meaning "Christ."

"The angel Gabriel was sent from God to a town of Galilee called Nazareth..." (Luke 1:26)

ST. MICHAEL THE ARCHANGEL
Feast Day September 29

Archangel Michael appears in Scripture twice each in the New Testament and three times in the old. He is a powerful warrior angel because he defeated the devil in battle. He protected heaven and protects us!

"Then war broke out in heaven; Michael and his angels battled against the dragon. The dragon and its angels fought back, but they did not prevail and there was no longer any place for them in heaven." (Revelation 12:7-9)

Patron of the Church, grocers, mariners, police officers, emergency medical technicians, soldiers and sick people

He is described in Holy Scripture as "one of the chief princes" and leader of the forces of heaven in their triumph over the powers of evil.

Sword for slaying the dragon

"At that time there shall arise Michael, the great prince, guardian of your people." (Daniel 12:1)

He is known as Protector of the Church.

Dressed in armor, ready for battle.

St. Michael

The name Michael means "Who is like God?"
He is one of the seven Archangels.
He is mentioned by name in Daniel, Jude and Revelation.

The prayer of St. Michael the Archangel is a powerful prayer. It is recommended we pray it every day to fight the forces of evil.

Prayer:
St. Michael the Archangel,
defend us in battle.
Be our defense against the wickedness and snares of the Devil.
May God rebuke him, we humbly pray,
and do thou,
O Prince of the heavenly hosts,
by the power of God,
thrust into hell Satan,
and all the evil spirits,
who prowl about the world
seeking the ruin of souls. Amen.

He is called the "Angel of Judgment" and holds scales in his hand to "weigh" the souls of the departed.

29

ST. THERESE OF LISIEUX
Feast Day October 1

St. Therese of Lisieux
Birth: January 2, 1873, in Alencon, France.
Death: September 30, 1897, in Lisieux, France
Canonized: by Pope Pius XI on May 17, 1925.

Patron saint of missions and missionaries

Therese was raised by devout parents, but her mother died when she was four years old. Her four older sisters helped take care of her. Therese attempted to enter the Carmelite convent of Lisieux first at age 9 and then again at 14, but was turned away both times because she was too young. She was so determined, she went to see the pope to ask his permission! The Holy Father told her to obey her superiors and that she would become a Carmelite if God willed it. To Therese's great delight, less than two months later, she was allowed to enter the Carmelite Convent.

By age 10 she had a great zeal and was confident that her life's mission was for the salvation of souls.

Baptized name: Marie-Francoise-Therese
Religious name: Sister Therese of the Child Jesus and the Holy Face
Nickname: "The Little Flower"

Her motto, "the little way," reminds us to strive for heaven by doing little things with great love and putting God and others first.
She practiced:
*Smiling and being charitable to someone who bothered her.
*Avoiding complaint and being grateful for the blessings of each day.
*Offering help to a friend when she preferred to do something else.

She is a Doctor of the Church!

She died at age 24 from tuberculosis, which was not treatable at that time. Her last words were: "My God, I love You!"

She loved attending the Holy Mass and felt most united to Jesus after receiving Him in the Eucharist.

She admired St. Joan of Arc and wrote two plays based on her life.

She wrote her life story in an autobiography titled "Story of a Soul."

Therese practiced making small sacrifices and acts of love to God each day. She would use a small string of beads in her pocket to keep track of them.

The first word she learned to read was "heaven".

"When I die, I will send down a shower of roses from the heavens. I will spend my heaven doing good on earth."
–St. Therese

She was a lively, mischievous and self-confident child with a deep prayer life.

30

St. Francis of Assisi

Birth: 1181 in Assisi, Umbria, Italy
Death: October 4, 1226 in Assisi
Canonized: July 16, 1228 by Pope Gregory IX

Francis was born to a wealthy, noble family and enjoyed worldy pleasures. He was handsome, charming and very popular. Francis dreamed of being a glorious knight. But on his way to battle, one night Francis had a dream in which God told him to return home. This drastically changed his life. He renounced his old life of money and fame and took up a life of complete poverty for the Lord. He sold everything he owned, lived outside and ministered to the poor, sick and suffering. Francis was exuberant with joy, living his life for the Lord.

Patron saint of animals, merchants, ecology and Assisi, Italy

Thanks to Francis, we have Nativity Scenes to display at Christmas! He created the first one, using real people and animals to recreate the scene of Jesus' birth.

Through his actions, Francis taught the importance of showing true honor and respect for all people.

Pope Francis chose his papal name after him!

"For it is in giving that we receive." –St. Francis

He was a deacon, not a priest.

Francis received a message from God to rebuild the Church. To do so, he taught people about the importance of conversion and obedience to God and the Church.

Characteristics of a Francisican Friar:
*tonsure hair cut
*long beard
*brown habit with a corded belt

He was the first person to receive the Stigmata, the wounds of Christ.

Francis became a vibrant preacher to both the rich and poor. He was even known to preach to birds!

Francis loved all animals and had a gift of taming the wildest beasts. After Francis spoke to a ferocious wolf that was threatening a town, the wolf had a change in temperament and became a gentle and loving animal to the townspeople.

Three knots for poverty, chastity, and obedience

He founded the Franciscan Order, and after just ten years, there were over 5,000 friars. Fransiscans take vows of Chastity, Poverty and Obedience.

ST. FRANCIS OF ASSISI
Feast Day October 4

ST. TERESA OF AVILA
Feast Day October 15

St. Teresa of Avila
Birth: March 28, 1515 in Avila, Spain
Death: October 4, 1582 in Alba de Tormes, Salamanca, Spain
Canonized: March 12, 1622 by Pope Gregory XV

Teresa was raised in Avila, Spain, a fortified city. She lived during the Spanish Inquisition. As a young girl, she loved God and adventure so much that, at the age of seven, she attempted to set out for a mission to convert nonbelievers outside of the city wall. Thankfully, her uncle stopped her before she could get hurt by the enemy soldiers.

Patron saint of Spain, headache sufferers, Catholic writers, bodily ills, Discalced Carmelites, and those ridiculed for their piety

Teresa was a mystic and Doctor of the Church.

She had a great sense of humor and a delightful personality.

When Teresa entered the Carmelite Order, she was disappointed because the cloistered sisters were living a luxurious life and not dedicated to prayer. She felt called to reform the order so that they lived holy lives, detached from worldly pleasures and devoted to Christ in the Sacraments and prayer.

Teresa is a model of perseverance. She believed that, from undergoing trials, one learns the depths of Christ's love.

Teresa was very close to her parents. When Teresa's mother died, she went before an image of the Blessed Mother and asked Mary to be her mother.

"Let nothing disturb you, nothing frighten you. All things pass. God does not change. Patience achieves everything. Whoever has God lacks nothing; God alone suffices"
—St. Teresa of Avila

She took the name "Teresa of Jesus" when she became a nun.

A quill pen for writing. Her book, "*The Interior Castle*," has influenced how people pray.

In her autobiography she shares both her struggles and joys in living a life for Christ.

Sts. John of the Cross and John of Avila were her friends!

She founded the Discalced Carmelites who wear a brown habit.

As children, Teresa and her brother enjoyed collecting rocks to build little churches in their yard.

St. John Paul II
Feast Day October 22

St. John Paul II
Birth: May 18, 1920 in Poland
Death: April 2, 2005 in Rome Italy
Canonized: April 27, 2014 by Pope Francis

John Paul II saw his country destroyed by Communism and experienced firsthand the fear of being a Christian under a government who persecuted the faithful. He lived through World War II and many difficult and sad times, but his father's holy example strengthened his faith and sparked his vocation to the priesthood. John Paul II studied for the priesthood in secret while working an arduous job under the Communist rule. His early experiences shaped him into a holy man. He had a special love for the youth and called them "the future of the Church." He had a way of touching the hearts of all people. He was a very loved priest, bishop, cardinal and pope.

- He traveled to 129 countries during his papacy.
- He could speak eleven languages.
- He had a phenomenal memory, and never forgot anyone he met.
- His favorite prayer was the rosary!
- Patron saint of youth, chastity, evangelization and missions
- The white zucchetto is worn only by a pope.
- He loved Divine Mercy devotions of St. Faustina and encouraged others to pray the Chaplet.
- He loved acting in plays as a young adult. He even wrote a play called "The Jeweler's Shop."
- He was the first Polish pope!
- He was canonized on Divine Mercy Sunday!
- He was an avid writer and taught about the true purpose and freedom of love, the importance of chastity, and respecting the dignity of the human person.
- As Holy Father, his papal vestments are white.
- Pectoral cross, keeping Christ close to his heart.
- His motto was Totus Tuus which in Latin means "totally yours", an expression of his consecration to Jesus through Mary.
- As a priest, he spent a week in Italy praying and confessing with St. Padre Pio, who predicted that he would one day be Pope.
- His birth name was Karol Wojtyla. His nickname was "Lolek."
- "Dear young people, let yourselves be taken over by the light of Christ, and spread that light wherever you are." –St. John Paul II
- He loved to hike, camp and ski!

ST. JUAN DIEGO
Feast Day December 9

St Juan Diego
Birth: 1474 Cuauhtitlan, Mexico
Death: May 30, 1548, in Tepeyac, Mexico
Canonization: July 31, 2002 by Pope John Paul II at the Basilica of Our Lady of Guadalupe in Mexico

Juan Diego lived during the time when Spain sent Franciscan missionaries to Mexico to evangelize the native people who had never heard the Gospel message. After he was baptized by the Franciscans, Juan Diego lived a simple life, working, caring for his sick uncle, praying and teaching the faith to others. He is remembered as the humble man to whom the Blessed Mother appeared under the title of Our Lady of Guadalupe.

Patron saint of indigenous people, evangelization

He loved the Holy Eucharist and would walk several miles to attend daily Mass.

The first appearance of Mary to Juan Diego was on December 9, 1531. While he was walking to church one morning, he heard music coming from the top of the hill and saw a woman, dressed like an Aztec princess, with a bright light shining around her. She called him by name and expressed her love for the people of Mexico. She sent him to tell the Bishop to build a church on that hill.

Juan Diego was a model of humility, courage and obedience.

He encountered obstacles along the way, but the Blessed Mother interceded on his behalf. Today the Basilica of Our Lady of Guadalupe stands on the very same hill where Juan Diego encountered Our Lady.

After the Blessed Mother arranged roses in Juan Diego's tilma, her image was miraculously imprinted on the cloth.

The tilma with the image of Our Lady of Guadalupe is in the basilica that was built on the same hill where Our Lady appeared.

Juan Diego was instrumental in evangelizing the indigenous people of Mexico.

Our Lady of Guadalupe

Apparition Date: December 9th-12th, 1531
Place of Apparition: Tepeyac Hill, Mexico (Present day Mexico City)

Our Lady first appeared to Juan Diego on Tepeyac Hill in Mexico, dressed like an Aztec princess. She asked him to go to the bishop and request that a chapel be built on the site where she appeared. She visited him there several times, bringing three miracles.
1. Juan Diego's dying uncle was healed.
2. Roses from Spain grew in the middle of winter for Juan Diego to carry to the bishop in his tilma (cloak).
3. Our Lady of Guadalupe's image appeared on his tilma when he presented the roses to the bishop.

Researchers from around the world are perplexed about how Our Lady's image appeared and has lasted over 500 years. There is absolutely no evidence of paint or stitching on the tilma, and it is considered a true miracle.

One research doctor heard a heartbeat coming from her image on the tilma.

Our Lady brought many people to Jesus through her apparition.

Patroness of the Americas and the unborn

Her pink dress and green mantle with gold trim are considered colors of royalty.

The stars on her mantle form the exact constellation that was visible in the sky on the night she appeared.

The pink shade of her dress matches the color of the dirt from the hill on which she appeared.

Black ribbon representing virginity. Its high placement represents that she is with child.

Mexico City is the most popular pilgrimage site in the Western Hemisphere.

Mary spoke to Juan Diego as a loving mother, referring to him as "my dear son."

Mary wants all people to know that she is the mother of God and our mother. She compassionately loves and cares for us. She desires to help us when we are sad or going through difficult times. She yearns to give us her divine Son and bring us closer to him.

OUR LADY OF GUDALUPE Feast Day December 12

ST. LUCY
Feast Day December 13

St. Lucy
Birth: 283 A.D. in Syracuse, Sicily (Italy)
Death: 304 A.D. in Syracuse

Patron saint of the blind and those with eye trouble

Her name means "light," and she is known as the "bearer of light."

Lucy dedicated her life to Christ. She encountered difficulties along the way. Where she lived, there was a powerful pagan man who wanted to marry her, and he was not happy when she refused to be his wife. He did not like that she was a Christian and reported her to the authorities, who were also pagan. They attempted to persuade Lucy to leave her faith and live a worldly life surrounded by sin, but she loved Jesus more than any wealth, power or pleasure that they could offer. Since Lucy refused to submit to the evil thoughts and doings of the pagan authorities, she died a martyr of the Faith.

God gave Lucy new eyes after hers were injured by people who were trying to make her give up her Christian faith. That is why she is often represented holding a gold platter with a pair of eyes.

Her name in Italian and Spanish is "Lucia."

Festivals of Light are a popular tradition celebrated on her feast day.

The Italians depict St. Lucy holding palm branches to remind us that she was a martyr and a set of eyes to show that she saw the world through the eyes of Christ.

In Scandinavia (Sweden, Norway, Denmark), St. Lucy is depicted in a white dress, with a red sash and a crown of candles on her head.

36

ST. JOHN THE EVANGELIST
Feast Day December 27

John was the son of Zebedee and Salome. He was considered the youngest apostle. He was about 25 years old when he met Jesus. He and his brother were nicknamed by Jesus as "Sons of Thunder" (Mark 3:17) which is believed to describe their strength, active faith and explosive way of evangelizing. They did not allow fear to hold them back in their mission to follow Jesus and spread the Good News.

St. John the Evangelist
Birth: approximately in the year 15 A.D. in Bethsaida, Galilee
Death: approximately in the year 100 A.D. in Ephesus (present day Turkey)

Though he was the youngest apostle, he lived into his 90s. Many ancient icons paint him as an older man like he is painted here.

Patron saint of friendship, book sellers, art dealers, printers and the country of Turkey

He was known as a zealous and courageous apostle.

He was a fast runner and was the first Apostle to arrive at the tomb after Mary Magdalene told them that Jesus' body was not there.

He is called the "Apostle of Charity"

John was fishing in the Sea of Tiberias with others when the risen Jesus appeared to them. John recognized Jesus by his love and told the others, "It is the Lord." After Jesus gave them fishing advice, He served John and the other men breakfast. (John 21:1-14)

He was a fisherman before Jesus called him to become His disciple.

His older brother was St. James the Greater (also an Apostle).

John is known as the beloved disciple of Christ, "the one whom Jesus loved."

He rejoiced in suffering for Christ and died a martyr of the faith.

He had the courage to stay with Jesus during the crucifixion, comforting Our Lady at the foot of the cross.

At Calvary, Jesus chose John to care for his mother, Mary after the crucifixion.

John wrote one of the four Gospels, Revelation and three Epistles of the New Testament. John begins the Gospel with, "In the beginning was the Word, and the Word was with God and the Word was God."

He was a missionary in Asia.

ABOUT THE AUTHOR/DESIGNER
Maggie & Michael Jetty

Michael Jetty, graphic & web designer, photographer, owner of MJ Designs, LLC (mjdesigns-llc.com)

Maggie Jetty, speech therapist, author and painter of Saintly Heart little wooden peg dolls (saintlyheart.com)

Confirmation saint: St. Michael the Archangel

Confirmation saint: St. Teresa of Avila

He graduated from Arizona State University with a degree in Graphic Information Technology

She graduated from San Diego State with a degree in Spanish and Linguistics & Northern Arizona University with a master's in Clinical Speech Language Pathology

Did mission work in the U.S., Mexico and the Virgin Islands through Youth Arise.

She did mission work in Tijuana, Mexico and Honduras while in college.

Attended World Youth Day three times – Rome, Toronto, & Cologne

Married in 2009 on the feast of Blessed Mother Teresa. Received a papal blessing in Rome from Pope Benedict XVI four days later!

Plays volleyball and basketball

They make their home in Arizona

Loves learning about the lives of saints!

Plays electric guitar and bass

They have two sweet, funny, active, loud, thoughtful, Jesus-loving boys.

Laptop for web design

They have many wonderful nieces, nephews and Godchildren.

Enjoys painting saints and other loved ones

Loves to cook!

Favorite prayers are the Holy Mass and rosary.

Born and raised in Texas by his loving parents.

They have served on two family missions in Spain through Catholics In Action of Cuenca.

She was born and raised in California by two loving parents and three older brothers.

Has 5 sisters and 1 brother!

They both attended World Worth Day 2002 in Toronto with St. Pope John Paul II before knowing each other. Perhaps God brought them together through that moment in time?

Blaise
Savio

We dedicate this book to our sons, Blaise and Savio. May the saints always be their friends, guiding them to heaven. All Glory to God!

Thank you to our pastor, Fr. Sergio, for guiding and encouraging us to grow closer to our heavenly friends.

The Rev. Sergio M. Fita
Servi Trinitatis

Encyclopedia of Peg Saints
Copyright © 2015 Maggie and Michael Jetty
Printed in the USA

First Edition
10 9 8 7 6 5 4 3 2 1
ISBN 978-1-940209-19-7

No part of this publication may be reproduced, stored in a retrieval system or transmitted in any form or by any means, electronic, mechanical, photocopying, recording or otherwise without written permission of the publisher.

Contact Sherry@LilyTrilogy.com
All saint images in the public domain via Wikimedia Commons
Peg saint photos by Saintly Heart
Back cover photo: Rome, Vatican city © TTstudio via Fotolia

CARITAS PRESS   CaritasPress.org

Caritas Press was founded in 2011 with the mission of shedding light on things eternal in a culture that is becoming increasingly blind to the wonders of God's works and numb to His boundless love. Making use of the subtle and the beautiful, Caritas Press hopes to play a part in igniting in children and adults a desire to know God more fully. For a full listing of all Caritas titles for children, youths and adults, visit CaritasPress.org.

A special thanks to Bishop Wall for his prayers, kindness and love for the saints.

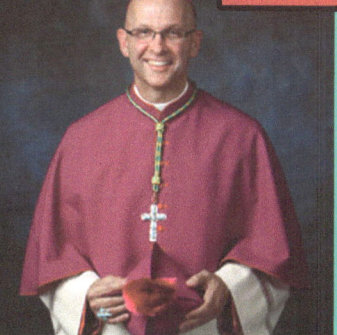

Most Reverend James S. Wall, Bishop of Gallup, New Mexico

Ordained a priest: June 6, 1998
Consecrated bishop: April 23, 2009

His pectoral cross has stones of turqouise representing his place of birth on the Navajo Nation in Arizona

SPECIAL THANK YOUS

Other children's books available from
CaritasPress.org and CatholicWord.com

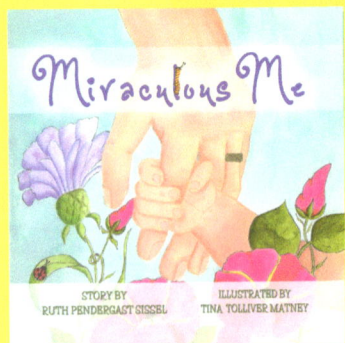

Miraculous Me
Ruth Pendergast Sissel and
Tina Tolliver Matney

Barnyard Bliss
Ruth Pendergast Sissel
and Tina Tolliver Matney

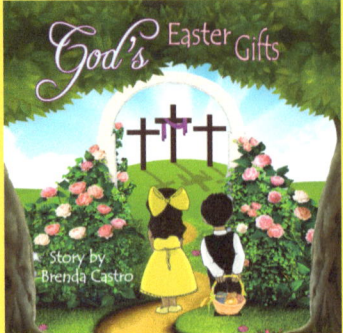

God's Easter Gifts
by Brenda Castro

Victoria's Sparrows
by Sherry Boas

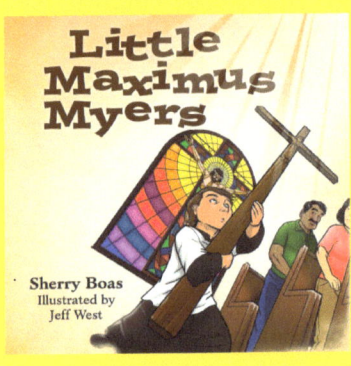

Little Maximus Myers
by Sherry Boas

Billowtail: A Novel
by Sherry Boas

**Saint John Bosco
and His Big Gray Dog**
by Hayley Medeiros

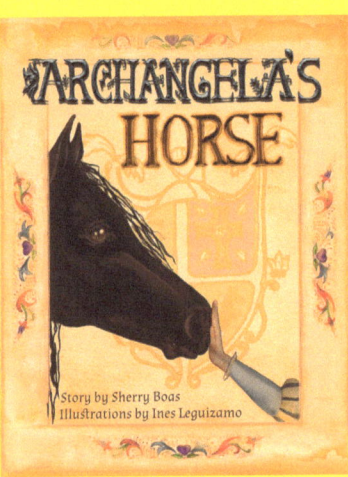

Archangela's Horse
by Sherry Boas and
Ines Leguizamo

The Gift in the Manger
by Sherry Boas

www.ingramcontent.com/pod-product-compliance
Lightning Source LLC
Chambersburg PA
CBHW040017050426
42451CB00002B/12